Sermon Analysis for Pulpit Power

Gateway Seminary Library

SERMON ANALYSIS FOR PULPIT POWER

H. C. Brown, Jr.

BROADMAN PRESS

Nashville, Tennessee

© Copyright 1971 • Broadman Press
All rights reserved

ISBN: 0–8054–2105–X
4221–05

Library of Congress Catalog Card Number: 72–145979
Dewey Decimal Classification: 251
7.5S7018

To all

of my student assistants

and graduate students

1949–1971

and especially to

those who have worked

with me on advancing

the development of

the sermon grading code

presented in this book

F. B. Huey
Lavon Brown
Bill Everett
Farrar Patterson
Gene Hadley
T. O. Spicer
Gordon Grimes
Al Fasol
Roy DeBrand

CONTENTS

Introduction

Part 1 Analyzing the Foundations of Your Sermon

Part 2 Analyzing the Construction of Your Sermon

Part 3 Analyzing the Final Factors of Your Sermon

Postscript

CONTENTS

INTRODUCTION

Preachers feel about their sermons the same way mothers feel about their babies! Preachers desire only praise for their sermons, as mothers desire only praise for their children. And rightly so! Why not?

H. H. Hobbs gave me this analogy years ago. He also said that sometimes one has grave difficulty knowing what to say about a particular sermon or a particular baby. He suggested that at such times a solution could be found only by saying, "My, what a baby!" Then the mother could make her own interpretation and application. One also must say at times, "My, what a sermon!"

All of us who preach know this feeling well. We have been on both sides of the issue. And it is preferable to be confused about what to say than to be confused about what has been said! At least it is for me.

Most preachers honestly desire to improve as pulpit servants. Most seek constructive and creative help from friends, fellow pastors, and foes alike. But such criticism comes costly. A preacher can hardly secure it from his friends and fellow pastors. What comes from foes—folks temporarily or permanently hostile—seldom measures up as creative or constructive. Criticism it is, but it is mostly negative!

A sabbatic leave program for ministers, if only for a vacation, a summer, or a semester, would be enormously beneficial. Just imagine the improvement in sermon preparation and delivery a minister could make by submitting himself, after years in hard pastorates, to the discipline of seminary preaching classes. In his more mature years—if his mind were open to true improvement—he could make unbelievable progress.

Since sabbatic leaves or extended leaves are not open to most ministers, this book represents a desire to bring the techniques and procedures of the seminary classroom to the preacher. This book offers self-analysis for sermon success. It shows a way for preachers to be more objective about their sermons, and hence more helpful to themselves, in the craft of constructing creative sermons. The term "self-analysis" as used in this book refers to homiletical rather than psychological self-analysis. This book makes it possible for a preacher to analyze a sermon *before he has preached it* in order that he may improve it in the preparation stage.

The basic plan of the book will be to ask the reader questions so that he can test himself. Proper explanations, applications, and illustrations are provided with the questions as standards for self-testing. The key test questions will be marked as Question 1, Question 2, until the end. Most, but not all, of the questions are designed to be answered either yes or no.

How many ways can you test or grade sermons? No one knows exactly, but there are at least eight:

1. You can test a sermon by a predetermined set of standards. These standards can be self-imposed, or they can be set out by teachers of preaching classes or by writers of preaching books.

2. You can test a sermon by its biblical authority. How close does the sermon come to explaning, illustrating, and applying the divine revelation contained in the text of the sermon?

3. You can test a sermon by its biblical purpose. How close does the sermon come to explaining, illustrating, and applying the intent or purpose of the text?

4. You can test for rhetorical form or mechanics. How close does the sermon come to the best grammatical and rhetorical standards for written composition prepared for oral delivery?

5. You can test by content. Content can be checked only by reading and analyzing each paragraph of explanation, argumentation, application, and illustration. On the negative side, content cannot be checked accurately by merely reading or hearing a sermon outline. The entire output of words determines content.

6. You can test for style. By long-standing consensus style in homiletics primarily relates to clarity, appeal, and force. How clear is the sermon? How much does it appeal to the hearers? How forceful is it?

7. You can test for oratorical or speech quality. How well does the preacher speak? Sermons are not meant to be merely prepared and read; they are also meant to be preached. The preacher should make use of the best principles of speech in the pulpit. Strangely enough, some ministers feel completely at liberty to disregard acceptable speech standards. The wisest preacher, however, rather than depreciating speech techniques, will make every effort to master them.

8. You can test by personal taste. This test says simply, "I like this sermon," or, "I do not like it." It says, "I like the preacher," or "I do not like him." This test is the most subjec-

tive and fallible; nevertheless, it is one valid test. It is the test applied by most people most of the time.

A suggested chronology for sermon preparation would be beneficial to many ministers. It is hereby set out for those who seek faster, more accurate, and more creative ways of constructing sermons.[1]

Step 1: The first step in sermon preparation involves a *prepared preacher*. The called man is one whom God has chosen to be his spokesman. Let the preacher look carefully to his conversion, call, and consecration.

Step 2: The second step involves *a usable idea*. This idea may come from various sources from time to time. The idea for the sermon should always be grounded in a text. Select a text to match your sermon idea.

Step 3: The third step involves *the correct interpretation of the text* which is wedded to the original idea. The two should become one. Moreover, this text ought to be studied until it yields its truth in three forms:

1. The central idea of the text (CIT)

2. The present-tense statement of the text (the thesis, proposition, or affirmation)

3. The purpose of the text

Purpose, as used homiletically, involves three stages:

1. Total purpose or the total goal for a man's ministry.

2. Major purposes or major goals which relate both to the text and the sermon. The six major purposes are the *evangelistic* (that lost persons trust Christ for salvation); the *doctrinal* (that Christians understand the Bible and God's truth); the *actional* (that Christians serve God with their time, talents, resources, and personality); the *ethical* (that

[1] See Brown, Clinard, and Northcutt, *Steps to the Sermon* (Nashville, Broadman Press, 1963).

Christians have a Christian relationship with others); the *devotional* (that Christians love and worship God); and the *supportive* (that Christians find strength and comfort for their troubles, trials, and tribulations).

3. A specific purpose for each sermon. The specific purpose is always one part of one major objective in one sermon to meet one audience need. The specific objective calls for the same audience response as the original biblical text.

Step 4: The fourth step in sermon preparation involves *the collection of all possible materials*—in the form of explanation, argumentation, application, and illustration—which may assist the preacher in the preparation of his sermon.

Step 5: The fifth step involves the proper *maturity of sermon materials.* Let the preacher start his sermon preparation early enough so that he can adequately mold his materials by the maturation process. Monday before the coming Sunday ought to be absolutely the latest time for starting a sermon.

Step 6: The sixth step—and the most complicated—requires that the preacher *organize or construct his message.* The work at this stage demands five activities: (1) the phrasing of a sermon title which will embrace the essence of all previous data; (2) the proper outlining and developing of the sermon body; (3) the construction of an appealing conclusion; (4) the writing of a clear and interesting introduction; (5) the preparation and listing of the invitation, or invitations, as needed.

Step 7: The seventh step in sermon preparation demands that the preacher *recheck, edit, correct, and polish* the entire sermon. This step relates directly to the style of the sermon. As you will recall, style relates directly to clarity, appeal, and force.

Step 8: The final step in sermon preparation calls for *preaching the sermon* in the power of the Holy Spirit.

Eight fundamental presuppositions undergird this book:

1. Preaching is the oldest and best God-ordained method for presenting the gospel.

2. Biblical preaching is the best kind of preaching. (The methodology of this book relates directly to the preparation of biblical sermons.)

3. Preaching can take many forms: the pulpit sermon, person-to-person witnessing, the written sermon, the radio sermon, the television sermon, and others. Moreover, drama, art, teaching, missions, evangelism, visual aids, movies, music, and other forms of oral and written communication can effectively present the gospel.

4. For men who are pastors of local churches, preaching is their primary work.

5. All ministers, whatever their particular vocational position, should acquire as much skill in preaching as possible.

6. Any preacher can improve his ability to preach by a careful study of preaching (homiletics).

7. Most minister-pastors will spend most of their available study-time preparing to preach. They should, therefore, learn the great principles of preaching.

8. Seminary disciplines (areas of study) have their best outlet through the pulpit for most ministers. Therefore, all minister-pastors should endeavor to focus all learning on producing creative and effective sermons.

Eight basic goals are involved in the study of preaching (homiletics). These eight goals are broader than this volume; they are simply listed here as guides for preachers who seek to improve their preaching skills. The eight great goals for a study of homiletics are: (1) that ministers learn the basic principles of preaching in order to prepare effective sermons; (2) that ministers learn the principles of biblical interpretation; (3) that ministers learn how to use the Old Testament and New Testament as dynamic sources for creative sermons; (4) that ministers learn the inspiring lessons about life, ministry, and preaching taught by great preachers and their preaching; (5) that ministers learn the principles of oral delivery; (6) that ministers learn the principles of effective, creative, and dynamic style (clarity, appeal, force) for sermons; (7) that ministers understand and preach on the great critical issues of the day; (8) that ministers learn to use all of life and its culture as content for effective sermons.

This brief book contains three simple parts, each of which has a few short chapters. Part 1 analyzes the foundations of the sermon; part 2 analyzes the construction of the sermon; part 3 analyzes the final factors of the sermon.

In form this book resembles a programmed course for pulpit progress. Questions are asked and answers supplied for the reader's assistance.

In using this book, picture yourself sitting at your desk with your sermon manuscript before you. The time probably is Saturday (or earlier), before you have preached your message. A manuscript represents the focus of attention for this reason: if you have prepared a sermon manuscript, you are probably well prepared to preach. Moreover, if you have a complete manuscript, you will be able to submit it to the tests set forth in this book. The focus of each key question in this book points to the preacher at his desk with his manuscript spread out before him. Most, but not all, questions asked in this planned check list can be answered by yes or no. If your answer to any of these questions is no, additional work and study are needed. Make your correction on the question answered no before you proceed to the next question.

Three basic books undergird this volume. For fuller analysis and discussion of any point, see the appropriate chapters in: *A Christian Layman's Guide to Public Speaking; Steps to the Sermon;* and *A Quest for Reformation in Preaching.*

How can you best use this book? Ten simple procedures are set out for your use in reading and applying it: (1) Read the book, marking all points which attract your attention. (2) Re-read the book, dwelling on the marked passages. (3) Prepare a sermon. (4) Go over your sermon, testing it with this book in hand. (5) If more insight is needed, study the book, think hard, and make needed corrections in your sermon. (6) If you feel you need more information than this book gives, study the appropriate chapters from the three books listed above. (7) Go through the entire sermon following this general procedure. (8) Make all necessary corrections. (9) On your next sermon put into practice all that you have learned from this book and the above three books. (10) Continue this program for a period of months, and you will find yourself making remarkable progress.

Why don't you begin testing your own sermons for pulpit progress as soon as you read this book? Why not indeed! Therefore, let us begin.

PART ONE

Analyzing the Foundations of Your Sermon

CHAPTER I

Your Basic Beliefs About Preaching

The minister who holds a low estimation of preaching will prepare and preach poor sermons. The man who holds a high estimation of preaching will grow and develop. He will preach better and better sermons. This book is designed basically for the man in the second group.

Question 1: What is your concept of preaching?

The definite view you hold in your mind about the true nature of preaching will determine to a considerable degree the quality of your preaching.

Preaching is a complex, all-inclusive theological task. It can never be merely rhetoric and oratory, as some men seem to think. What, then, is preaching?

1. Preaching involves the accurate use of biblical materials.

2. Preaching requires the correct use of hermeneutical principles.

3. Preaching demands a valid, all-inclusive theological viewpoint.

4. Preaching involves a deep psychological understanding of the audience.

5. Preaching requires the best use of rhetoric for the production of sermons for oral delivery.

6. Preaching demands the pleasing use of oratory for excellent pulpit delivery.

Again, what is *your* concept of preaching?

Answer carefully, preacher, because your preaching performance depends greatly on your high or low estimation of your task.

Think high and preach well!

Think low and preach poorly!

It really is this simple!

CHAPTER II

Your Bible Study Habits

Why should you use the Bible in preaching? Why should sermons have texts?

The answer to both questions is that God has revealed much of his will to us through the Bible. It is the only source known to the preacher, the church, and the individual Christian where divine revelation can be found spelled out in human language about the deeds of God through the lives of chosen men. If the preacher desires to preach divine revelation, he must go to the Bible.

Question 2: What is the nature and state of your Bible study habits?

This question refers to Bible study habits for sermon preparation.

Is there a pattern of Bible study conducive to fruitful pulpit work? Yes, there are several such patterns. The following schedule presents one effective procedure:

1. In Bible study for sermon preparation, the first task is to locate the text for the occasion. The original sermon idea may start with a Scripture text. If so, the original idea and text are the same. The sermon idea, however, may begin in a nonbiblical framework, such as the needs of the people, a

planned program of preaching, the life and experiences of the preacher, or a flash of insight and inspiration.

Your task, when the original idea starts in a nonbiblical setting, is to locate and correlate. You must locate a Scripture passage which accurately portrays your idea, and you must test your Bible passage to be sure that it and the original idea match—that is, that they are properly correlated.

2. After you have an original idea and a text, read the text over and over in your favorite Bible translation (or translations). There is no substitute for knowing exactly what your text says.

3. Next, read your text over and over in a number of other Bible versions. Various versions have different emphases. You can learn much about your text by reading it in numerous Bible translations.

4. Think, meditate, and pray "without ceasing" about your text. Live with your text until it "lives with you!" Saturate yourself with the text.

5. Interpret the text for yourself. Do this by stating *in writing* what you believe to be the meaning of each verse. Also, try to state the meaning of your entire text by phrasing that meaning in one short declarative sentence. This sentence is called the *central ideal of the text* (CIT); it is also called the historical thesis.

Keep in mind that you should take these first five steps in Bible study before you turn to specific research in technical books. Many ministers feel that they are more susceptible to the leading of the Holy Spirit if they do intensive personal interpretation before they turn to books by scholars. This view is probably correct for a large number of preachers.

6. Finally, turn to the best research books available. If you live within reach of a college, university, or seminary, make

full use of the library resources there. If you are not close to a good library, purchase your own basic books for Bible research.

For most ministers, scholarly and technical books which give the true grammatical-historical-theological meaning of the Scriptures have more value than do devotional-practical books. You need not select one over the other, however, because you can use both. But be sure that you discover the true grammatical-historical-theological meaning of your text. You cannot preach truly biblical sermons without a real understanding of Scripture as God gave it "then."

The grammatical-historical-theological method of Bible study requires a careful analysis of eight factors. These are: (1) the historical facts intertwined with the text; (2) the accurate grammatical meaning of the words and sentences; (3) the proper theological meaning of the text set in the framework of all Scripture; (4) the lexical or dictionary meaning of all key words; (5) the cross-reference factor, in which related Scripture passages are checked against the text; (6) the rhetorical or literary factor, which clarifies the type of literature in the text under study; (7) the homiletical or practical factor, which discovers the eternal truth for the audience; and (8) the spiritual factor, which seeks divine aid in the interpretation of the text.

Notice question 2 again: What is the nature and state of your Bible study habits? If you do not have strong, effective, creative Bible study habits, your first task is to learn to study the Bible in this way.

CHAPTER III

Your Preliminary Homiletical Guides

As a navigator uses the stars as points of reference for navigation, the minister must use certain preliminary or basic homiletical items as points of reference in order to prepare sermons correctly. There are six such preliminary guide items which must be prepared and closely followed in order to produce creative and effective sermons. These items are called *preliminary or basic guide items* because they serve as the structure around which the words of the sermon are phrased for completeness. These six guide items are to a sermon what the skeleton steel structure is to a building.

1. The biblical text (part of step two in sermon preparation)
2. The central idea of the text—always written in past tense in order to convey the original meaning of the text (part of step three)
3. The thesis—a present-tense statement of the central idea of the text (part of step three)
4. The purpose—the intent of the Scripture text (part of step three)
5. The title—the essence or total of the first four items (part of step six)

6. The points of the sermon body, drawn simultaneously from the title and the text (part of step six)

These six items should be prepared as part of steps 2, 3, 4, 5, and 6. The order of preparation, you will recall, is as follows:

Step 1: the preparation of the preacher

Step 2: the location of a sermon idea and text

Step 3: the interpretation of the text so as to produce a CIT (central idea of the text), thesis (a present-tense statement of the CIT), and purpose (both major and specific)

Step 4: the collection of all possible creative content in the form of explanation, argumentation, application, and illustration

Step 5: the maturity of all sermon materials

Step 6: the writing of a title from all the above items and the stating of body points which develop the title, text, and other preliminary items

The other sermon items belonging to step 6 (conclusion, introduction, and invitation) will be discussed later.

Question 3:   Does your central idea of the text accurately state the meaning of the Scripture as God gave it?

The central idea of the text should be stated in a simple declarative sentence in past tense, using fifteen words or less. It should reveal the dominant thought of the text under study. There are five short but important checks for the CIT:

1. Have you written the CIT in the form of a simple declarative sentence of fifteen or less words?

2. Have you written the CIT in past tense?

3. Have you written the CIT so as to state the central and true historical meaning of the total text?

4. Have you written the CIT so that it is stated clearly, appealingly, and forcefully?

5. Have you written the CIT so that it includes only biblical information?

All five answeres should be yes. If the answer to one or more of these questions is no, go back and repair your statement of the CIT.

Question 4: Does your thesis (or proposition or affirmation) accurately translate the central idea of the text to present-tense meaning?

The thesis should be stated in a simple declarative sentence in present tense, using fifteen words or less. The thesis should reveal the dominant thought of the text under study as it relates to present-day life. You may use these five checks for the thesis:

1. Have you written the thesis in the form of a simple declarative sentence of fifteen or less words?

2. Have you written the thesis in present tense?

3. Have you written the thesis so as to state the central and true present meaning of the text?

4. Have you written the thesis so that it is stated clearly, appealingly, and forcefully?

5. Have you written the thesis so that it includes only biblical information?

If the answer to one or more of the checks is no, go back and repair the thesis. Remember, each question here should be answered by a yes.

Question 5: Does your sermon purpose (both major and specific) accurately convey the true intent and purpose of the text?

The *major purpose* should be one of these six: evangelistic, doctrinal, ethical, devotional, actional, or supportive. The major purpose is best stated by one word. It should always reflect a major need of the audience. The *specific purpose* should be one subdivision of one major purpose which calls for decision according to the intent of the text. The specific purpose is best stated in one sentence of fifteen words or less and should reflect an urgent audience need. You may use these checks to determine whether your specific purpose is accurately stated:

1. Have you written the specific purpose in the form of a simple declarative sentence of fifteen or less words?

2. Have you written the specific purpose in present or future tense form?

3. Have you written the specific purpose so as to call for action according to the intent of the text?

4. Have you written the specific purpose so that it is stated in a clear, appealing, and forceful manner?

5. Have you written the specific purpose so that it includes only biblical intent or biblical purpose?

If the answer to any one of the checks is no, go back and repair the purpose—major or specific—as needed. Remember that if the major purpose is not correct, the specific purpose cannot be. Prepare each item so that it can be answered by yes.

Question 6: Does your sermon title accurately convey the meaning of the text, CIT, thesis, and purpose?

The title, when correctly stated, is the name of the sermon. It should reveal the whole of the previously treated items.[1]

The title should use from two to ten words, with not more than four strong words. It may be phrased in one of five basic word forms: the emphatic, the question, the sentence or declarative, the imperative, and the restricted. The

[1] See *A Christian Layman's Guide to Public Speaking* (Nashville: Broadman Press, 1967) for a simple explanation of these types of titles.

fifth form restricts itself to one of five basic forms in order not to usurp all the other forms. The restricted word form uses a specific number in the title, or the possessive case, or a comparative degree of an adjective, or the superlative degree, or an adverb in a place of prominence. The title should use *one* of these five basic forms (with five subcategories of the fifth form). These titles in print or on paper appear as follows (with key words in italics):

1. *The Emphatic Word Form*
   The *Power* of Prayer
   The *Divinity* of Jesus

2. *The Question Word Form*
   How Can You Pray with Power?
   How Could the Divine Son of God Be Human?

3. *The Sentence or Declarative Word Form*
   Prayer Has Power
   Jesus Is Lord of All

4. *The Imperative or Command Word Form*
   Pray Without Ceasing
   Believe on Jesus as Lord

5. *The Restricted or Limiting Word Form*
   The *Two* Natures of Jesus (a number used)
   Our *Lord's* Humanity (possession shown)
   Better Ways to Pray (comparative degree of adjective)
   The *Best* Way to Pray (superlative degree of adjective)
   When Prayers Are Not Answered (adverb)

The tests for the title are these:

1. Which type of title have you used?

2. Is the title biblical?

3. Is the style pleasing (clear, appealing, forceful)?

4. What is the key word in the title?

5. Have you developed the key word of the title in the sermon body?

If you cannot answer all these questions accurately, go back and repair your sermon title.

Question 7: *Does your sermon body accurately divide your title, text, and other preliminary items at the same time?*

The sermon is a unit, and the sermon body should show this unity. Almost all sermon bodies can be constructed with only Roman or major points. As a rule do not go beyond the subdivisions of the Roman points.

There are seven brief checks for the points of the sermon body:

1. Have you phrased your points as complete sentences?

2. Do the sermon points develop the key word of the title?

3. Are the sermon points phrased with uniform grammatical structure?

4. Is the style of the points clear, appealing, forceful?

5. Is a clear-cut line of thought revealed in each point?

6. Is the grammatical tense of the sermon body points consistent—each consistent with the others and all consistent with the sermon title?

7. Are the persons, places, and things from the title used consistently in the body points?

If you prepare and check out the six basic guide items for a sermon (see items listed on pp. 25-26) in connection with the sermon body points, your sermon will be a straight-line development from original idea to completed sermon. If you have only one guide point, you cannot draw a clear line of development. If you have six guidelines, you can accurately plot the course of the entire sermon.

Consider this: You start with an *idea* and *text;* draw the CIT from the *text;* phrase the *thesis* from the CIT; draw the *purpose* from all three; then construct the *title* from all four; and build the *sermon body* points from all five.

Now you can draw a tight straight line from original idea and text right through the sermon body. The task of completing all details is made easier if the line of development is straight and clear. Try it. It works.

In Part 1 you have been asked seven major questions and a number of minor questions. How are you doing thus far? If you are not satisfied, go back to study, meditate, think, and try again. The effort will be rewarding to you as you find yourself able to give correct answers to these questions.

PART TWO

Analyzing the Construction of Your Sermon

CHAPTER IV

Your Introduction

There are three primary purposes for the introduction: (1) to create interest in the message; (2) to introduce the sermon with clarity; (3) to establish rapport between preacher and audience.

The preliminary or basic guide items for the sermon find their best use, as a whole, in the introduction. The preacher has the challenging task of weaving his words together so as to present the text, the CIT, and the thesis; to set forth the purpose; and to state the title. In doing so the minister should use appealing opening sentences and creatively bridge the gap from introduction to sermon body. Every part of the introduction must be prepared with effective style.

There are numerous check questions for the introduction. For the sake of simplicity they are divided into categories.

Questions for the Text

Question 8: Has the text been prepared for presentation somewhere in the introduction?

Question 9: Has the text been prepared to be announced in this order: Bible book, chapter, and verse or verses?

Question 10: Will the Bible version used be made clear to the audience? (If you change versions from time to time in your preaching, always identify the version you are using.)

Question 11: Has careful thought been given to presenting the text wih clarity and appeal?

Question 12: Has the text been read orally many times in private in order to secure a good public reading of the Bible?
Answers to all these questions should be yes.

Questions for the Central Idea of the Text

Question 13: Has the CIT been prepared for presentation to the audience somewhere in the introduction?

Question 14: Has the CIT been written in past tense, as is befitting a true historical thesis?

Question 15: Has the CIT been written in a simple declarative sentence of fifteen words or less?

Question 16: Has the CIT been written as an accurate interpretation of the text?

Question 17: Has the CIT been written with clarity, appeal, and force?
Answers to all these questions should be yes.

Questions for the Thesis

Question 18: Has the thesis been prepared for presentation somewhere in the introduction?

Question 19: Has the thesis been written as a present-tense application of the text and CIT?

Question 20: Has the thesis been written as a simple declarative sentence of fifteen words or less?

Question 21: Has the thesis been written with clarity, appeal, and force?

Answers to all these questions should be yes.

Questions for the Purpose

Many ministers choose to present both the major and specific purposes for the sermon—*if they present them at all*—in the conclusion rather than the introduction. Keep in mind that the presentation of the purpose, especially for the introduction, is optional, as you test your purpose.

Question 22: Has the specific objective been written as a true specific objective?

Question 23: Does the specific objective set forth the same intent as the original text?

Question 24: Has the specific objective been written in a concise way with a strong verb calling for action?

Question 25: Has the specific objective been written with clarity, appeal, and force?

Answers to all these questions should be yes.

Questions for the Title

It seems, at times, as if each speaker in the world who tries to communicate with people shares with these people what he is trying to communicate—everyone, that is, except the preacher! For some strange reason, preachers often refuse to present their titles to their congregations. Many answers to this criticism are given, some facetious and some serious. One student gave this facetious reason: "If I gave my title, the people would expect me to preach on it!" This simple joke comes close to the truth as to why some preachers never reveal their sermon titles.

Question 26: Has the sermon title been written for presentation somewhere in the introduction?

Question 27: Has the sermon title been written with clarity, appeal, and force?

Question 28: Has the title been written with freshness and attractiveness, yet without cheap sensationalism?

Question 29: Has the sermon title been framed from the totality of the text, the CIT, the thesis, and the purpose?

Question 30: Has the title been phrased with a key word which can be developed in the sermon body?

Question 31: Has the title been written with from two to ten words, with not more than four strong words?
Answers to all these questions should be yes.

Questions for the Opening Sentences

Question 32: Has the first sentence you plan to speak been worked out carefully so as to have clarity, appeal, and force?

Question 33: Have the first few sentences of the introduction been written as relatively short ones?

Question 34: Have you considered varying the opening sentences from sermon to sermon by using the preliminary guides (the text, the CIT, the thesis, the purpose, and the title) in different orders?
All of these questions should be answered yes.

Questions for the Transition Sentences

Question 35:   Have you worked out a smooth, effective transition from introduction to sermon body by using clarity, appeal, and force?

Question 36:   Have you used a fairly short sentence as the last or bridge sentence from introduction to the sermon body?

Question 37:   Have you actually tied your introduction and sermon body together by your transition sentences?
Answers to all of these questions should be yes.

General Questions for the Introduction

Question 38:   Has the introduction been written so as to use about 10 to 20 percent of the total time for the message?

Question 39:   Has the style (clarity, appeal, and force) of the entire introduction been written with care?

Question 40:   Have the basic homiletical guides been used carefully and creatively in the introduction?
Answers to all these questions should be yes.

CHAPTER V

Your Sermon Body

The sermon body will be examined from two broad perspectives: the sermon body *outlined and organized;* and the sermon body *developed* by the functional elements.

Questions Concerning the Outline and Organization of the Sermon Body

Question 41: *Have the correct outline mechanics been used?*

The basic mechanics are these:

1. The major points of the sermon should use Roman numerals for identification.

2. The subdivisions of the major points should use Arabic numerals (1,2,3) or capital letters (A,B,C) as marks of identification.

3. Illustrations which clarify points should not be numbered separately from the points.

4. Scriptures in addition to the text (which support or clarify the text) should not be numbered separately from the points.

5. The functional elements of preaching (paragraphs of explanation, argumentation, and application) should not be numbered separately from the points which they develop.

6. The major parts of the sermon proper (the introduction, sermon body, conclusion, and invitation) should not be numbered in the outline of the sermon.

Question 42: Does each point (major point, subpoint, or sub-subpoint) which is divided have at least two parts? (However, the points do not have to be divided in order to be used. It is the preacher's choice as to whether a point is to be divided.)

Question 43: Does each subpoint actually divide the point above it? Do the major points actually divide the title?

Question 44: Does each major point show up clearly in the sermon body in the manuscript?

Question 45: Has the Scripture passage which produced each sermon point been identified with that point?

Question 46: Has the order of the sermon points been carefully checked?

Question 47: Has each sermon point been written as a complete sentence? (For the sake of clarity and completeness, it should be.)

Question 48: Have the sermon points been written in a consistent grammatical form? (For the sake of the audience's understanding, they should be.)

Question 49: Have the clarity, appeal, and force of each outline point been tested and polished?

Question 50: Does the grammatical tense of each sermon point match the tense or time shown in the sermon title?

Question 51:   Do the persons, places, and things of the sermon points match the same things in the title?

Question 52:   Does each sermon point have a clear line of direction (in order to facilitate further dividing or developing)?

Answers to all of these questions should be yes.

Questions Concerning the Body Development of the Functional Elements

The basic preliminary items of the sermon—text, central idea of the text, thesis, purpose (both major and specific), and title—should be properly treated and made clear in the body of the sermon.

The functional elements of the sermon are explanation, application, and argumentation. These are best set forth in separate paragraphs since there are a number of subcategories for each functional element.

By the process of *explanation* the preacher clarifies his sermon content. The preacher explains by one or more of these methods: (1) exposition, (2) division into points, (3) narration, (4) description, (5) argument, (6) illustration, (7) comparison, (8) contrast, (9) comparison and contrast, (10) questions and answers, (11) cross-reference to other Scripture passages. The basic questions to ask about *explanation* are these:

Queston 53:   Does the content of each paragraph of explanation actually explain?

Question 54:   Does each paragraph of explanation use the subcategories (listed above) correctly?

Question 55:   Does each paragraph of explanation use the grammatical tense best suited to the data being treated? (Past tense is the best tense for most explanatory paragraphs. Present-tense explanation is acceptable if done consistently with text, title, and point under consideration. However, the past tense is usually best for explanation of Scripture.)

Question 56: Has each paragraph of explanation been written with clarity, appeal, and force?

Question 57: Has each paragraph of explanation used the correct grammatical person (first, second, or third) to develop the point under consideration?
Answers to all of these questions should be yes.

The preacher *applies* his message by one or more of the following methods: (1) by *affirming* that the sermon truths relate or apply; (2) by showing *how* the sermon applies; (3) by showing *why* the hearer should act on the message; (4) by showing *when* the hearer should act; (5) by showing the *results* of acting; (6) by showing various *areas* or types of action; (7) by *exhorting* the hearer to act; (8) by extending an open *invitation* to act on the message.

Question 58: Does the content of each paragraph of application actually apply to the hearers?

Question 59: Does each paragraph of application correctly use one or more of the subcategories of application?

Question 60: Does each paragraph of application use the grammatical tense which best suits the data used? (The present tense is the normal tense for application. Some types of application call for the future tense.)

Question 61: Has each paragraph of application been written with clarity, appeal, and force?

Question 62: Has each paragraph of application used the correct grammatical person (first, second, or third) to develop the point under consideration?

Answers to all of these questions should be yes.

The preacher reasons or "argues" about his sermon material by one or more of the following methods: (1) by using argument from testimony; (2) by arguing from inference; (3) by using special forms of argument—*a priori; a posteriori; a fortiori;* dilemma; *ex concesso;* concept of progress; *reductio ad absurdem; ad hominem;* (4) by refutation; (5) by the natural development of an assertion.

Question 63: Does the content of each paagraph of argumentation actually reason or logically analyze the data under view?

Question 64: Does each paragraph of argumentation correctly use one or more of the subcategories of argumentation?

Question 65: Does each paragraph of argumentation use the grammatical tense best suited to the data used? (The present tense is the normal tense for argumentation.)

Question 66: Has each paragraph of argumentation been written with clarity, appeal, and force?

Question 67: Has each paragraph of argumentation used the correct grammatical person (first, second, or third) to develop the point under consideration?

Answers to all of these questions should be yes.

The illustration is a true servant of the three functional elements of explanation, application, and argumentation. Remember that the word "illustration" means "to il-lustrate"—to light up something. Because the work of an illustration is to "cast light" on other material, it is a servant of that other material. The preacher should clarify his content paragraphs of explanation, application, and argumentation by throwing light on them as needed.

Question 68: Has the illustration been presented directly without a formal or mechanical "gimmick" such as "Allow me to illustrate"? (The correct method is to illustrate without talking about the mechanics.)

Question 69: Has the nature of the illustration been made clear in its presentation? (Illustrations by nature are fact, fiction, opinion, preacher-created incidents, poetry, or prose. The preacher should identify for the audience the nature of the illustration. This identification should be given simply and briefly.)

Question 70: Has the source of the illustration been revealed? (Most of the time, the source should be identified in order to authenticate the illustration. This identification should be given simply and briefly. However, the preacher should not reveal confidential information without prior approval or without changes being made which will protect all persons involved. Preachers who violate this rule often have cause for regret.)

Question 71: Has the illustration been written with clarity, appeal, and force?
Answers to all of these questions should be yes.

CHAPTER VI

Your Sermon Conclusion

Question 72: Does the conclusion clearly reveal and stress the specific purpose of the sermon?

Question 73: Has the conclusion been written without new material being given to the audience? (The conclusion should be written without new or additional material. However, fresh illustrations do not count as additional material, since they merely illuminate other content.)

Question 74: Has careful use been made of the functional elements in the conclusion? (They should be used with great care in the conclusion. Application, normally, is the best functional element for the conclusion.)

Question 75: Does the conclusion comprise about five percent of the total sermon content?

Question 76: Does your conclusion really end the sermon in a way satisfying to the audience and to you?

Question 77: Does your conclusion prepare the way for an easy transition to the invitation? (You may state your invitation or invitations in the conclusion, if you wish, and, at the time of the invitation, give the people an opportunity to act or decide. The normal procedure, however, is to give the conclusion in such a way that it leads naturally to the invitation.)

Answers to all of these questions should be yes.

CHAPTER VII

Your Sermon Invitation(s)

Modern homiletics uses four parts for a sermon: introduction, body, conclusion, and invitation or invitations. In older preaching theory, the sermon invitation was treated as something apart from the sermon—if it was treated at all. But the sermon invitation must be considered a vital part of a well-prepared sermon. The invitation should be formulated during step six in sermon preparation and should be based directly on the specific purpose. (Review the previous data on sermon purpose, if necessary, for a proper understanding of the sermon invitation.)

The invitation is the part of the sermon during which the preacher challenges the people present to make a decision or decisions. The decision called for should grow out of the text, CIT, thesis, and major purpose. The first sermon invitation should always match the specific purpose.

Question 78: Have you written out your sermon invitation(s) in advance as part of step six? (You should always do so in order that you and your audience may know exactly what decisions are desired.)

Question 79: Have you written out clear transitional sentences to carry you from invitation to invitation, when you have more than one? (Prepare the first invitation in line with the specific purpose. Prepare proper transitional sentences to your other invitations.)

Question 80: Have you used your specific objective as your first invitation? (You should always do so.)

Question 81: Do you know exactly what you wish each one present to decide or to do?

Question 82: Have you decided when, where, and how those present can respond to your invitation(s)?

The audience can respond in at least four ways:

(1) They can come forward to make some type of public commitment—a profession of faith, a surrender to church-related vocation, a transfer of church membership, or a dedication of themselves to a better Christian life.

(2) They can decide privately in their hearts to change their lives for the glory of God—a decision known only to God and the individual.

(3) They can decide to go out into the world and take Christian action pleasing to God.

(4) They can seek out the pastor for a conference after the service or make an appointment for a later date. At the time of the conference, they can seek specific answers on how to make proper decisions.

The preacher should be able to answer yes to questions 78–82.

PART THREE

Analyzing the Final Factors of Your Sermon

CHAPTER VIII

Your Sermon Authority

The ideal in preaching is twofold: (1) The preacher should reproduce God's authentic message in modern rhetorical sermonic form. (2) He should deliver the message in the power of the Holy Spirit to people willing to hear God speak. When these conditions are met in one sermon through one preacher to one audience, authentic authoritative preaching takes place.

The more closely the sermon equals the eternal truth of the text and meets the immediate need of the audience, the closer the sermon comes to being truly biblical. One of the intriguing quests of modern homiletics is to develop a method of testing sermons to determine their biblical authority. One attempt to set out a procedure for testing the authority of a sermon is found in *A Quest for Reformation in Preaching*. The same procedure will be used in this book.

Sermons may be classified in five groups according to authority: (1) Sermons which develop the CIT as God gave it are *direct biblical sermons*. (2) Sermons in which the preacher adds something to the text (by completing an implication, by drawing a specific idea from a general truth, or by comparing or contrasting general ideas with text ideas) are *indirect biblical sermons.* (3) Sermons which develop a loose or a casual idea from the text are *casual biblical sermons.* (4) Sermons which abuse or mistreat the text are *corrupt biblical sermons.* (5) Sermons which treat some combination of these first four are *combination biblical sermons.*

Preachers throughout Christian history have preached all five of these sermon types. Likewise, preachers today use all five. The best sermon type is the direct biblical sermon. It should be the basic model for most if not all preachers.

Question 83: Have you reproduced the true central idea of the text in your sermon? (If you have, you probably have produced a *direct biblical sermon.* Normally this is the best type of sermon because the sermon says the same thing that the text says.)

Question 84: Have you departed slightly from the true central idea of the text in your sermon by completing an implication of the text, by drawing out a specific idea from a general truth of the text, or by comparing or contrasting ideas from the text? (The key point in this type of sermon is whether the preacher adds to, draws from, or uses comparison or contrast in the treatment of the text. This type of sermon is an *indirect biblical sermon,* because it contains some portion of "preacher-originated" basic content.)

Question 85: Have you prepared your sermon with only a loose relationship to your text? (If you have, you have prepared a *casual biblical sermon.* This type of sermon usually develops the title independent of a close and true relationship to the text.)

Question 86:   Have you changed or corrupted the central idea of the text? (This can be done by one of the following means: (1) allegorizing the meaning of the text; (2) treating the text carelessly without knowing what it means; (3) denying or rejecting the supernatural element in the text; (4) twisting the text to fit modern cultural and social views; (5) changing the text to fit denominational perspectives; (6) using the text to prove one's personal doctrines; (7) using the text as a scientific treatise; (8) pressing the loose casual treatment of the text so far that the real text has no relationship to the content of the sermon; (9) treating the text in a rigid, inflexible, wooden manner. If you have used your text in any of these ways, the chances are excellent that you have corrupted it. All these faults should be carefully avoided. In this type of sermon you will have a faulty or corrupted authority.)

Question 87:   Have you used a combination of any of the above-stated four types of biblical authority in your sermon? (If so, you have a *combination biblical sermon.* If some type of corruption of the text has been used, by all means eliminate it.)

The first three types of authority—direct, indirect, and casual—are all legitimate. In order of importance these types rank as follows: (1) direct, (2) indirect, and (3) casual. The fourth type—combination—fits into this ranking according to the way it is put together.

Try at all times to have the purest, most direct form of authority available to you. Check the biblical authority of your sermon carefully.

CHAPTER IX

Your Sermon Purpose

Preachers use purpose in sermons to indicate one of two things: (1) the purpose of the sermon or (2) the purpose of the text. Really, there should be only one use of purpose in preaching. The preacher should know the purpose or intent of his text so thoroughly that he makes the purpose of the text the purpose of his sermon. The sermon is strengthened by having one purpose for both text and sermon.

Nevertheless, even though purpose in preaching is singular, it has three degrees: (1) the total purpose of a minister for his entire ministry; (2) the major purpose for one sermon; and (3) the specific purpose, or course of action desired in one sermon. In order to have an effective sermon, all three degrees of purpose need to be used correctly. Therefore, recheck your uses of purpose.

Recheck Your Total Purpose

Question 88: Has your sermon been prepared so that people can find God's kind of life as a result of your sermon? (They should be able to do so.)

The total purpose for preaching is that the people have LIFE—life eternal and life abundant. The preacher should preach about issues and ideas which will make it possible for his people to have life. The preacher should always ask himself, "Can one or more persons in my congregation find *life* in my message?" This life eternal or life abundant must come from God. The preacher's task is to preach in such a way that people can find God's kind of life. Check carefully your *total* purpose.

Recheck Your Major Purpose

Question 89: Have you prepared your major purpose so that it matches the purpose or intent of the text? (Only one major purpose should be used for each sermon.)

The Scriptures set out six broad or major purposes. The preacher should understand these and make effective use of them in his sermon. The six major purposes of Scripture are these: (1) the evangelistic purpose (that lost men be saved); (2) the doctrinal purpose (that men understand the Bible and the truth about God); (3) the devotional purpose (that Christians love, worship, and adore God); (4) the ethical purpose (that Christians have a correct ethical or moral relationship with other persons or with institutions); (5) the actional purpose (that Christians serve God with their time, talent, personalities, and resources); and (6) the supportive purpose (that men find and use God's grace in the face of troubles, trials, and tribulations). It is best to have only one major purpose in a sermon.

Recheck Your Specific Purpose

Question 90: Have you prepared your specific purpose so that it is a true subcategory of one major purpose? (You should.)

See above in previous chapters, where five basic questions are set out which will aid your use of specific purpose.

These five questions are as follows:

1. Have you written the specific purpose in the form of a simple declarative sentence of fifteen or less words?

2. Have you written the specific purpose in present or future tense form?

3. Have you written the specific purpose so as to call for action according to the intent of the text?

4. Have you written the specific purpose so that it is stated in a clear, appealing, and forceful manner?

5. Have you written the specific purpose so that it includes only biblical intent or biblical purpose?

In concrete terms specific purpose is the one purpose or objective for one speaker in one sermon to one audience on one occasion. The preacher should always desire that decisions be made when he speaks. (See above for the multiple ways people can make decisions.)

CHAPTER X

Your Sermon Form

Preachers as a group tend to feel that there is a divinely inspired, "handed down," sermonic form which must be followed in order for a sermon to be "homiletical"! Occasionally a talented and creative preacher, in reaction to this idea, has said, "Brother, I can preach, but I throw homiletics out the window!" He cannot do so, of course. *You cannot preach at all if you throw homiletics out the window.*

Many laymen and young preachers, commenting about a favorite preacher, will say, "He is a great preacher, but he doesn't know a thing about homiletics." This statement, also, is incorrect. No preacher can be a strong preacher without being a good homiletician. He may have his own form of homiletics, but he will use homiletics if he preaches well! People who make statements like the ones quoted mean, *I think,* that the preachers in question move men with their preaching but that they do not follow the particular principles of great men of homiletics. These great teachers and authors of preaching materials would include John A. Broadus, Phillips Brooks, and Andrew Blackwood. (Music has its three *B*'s: Brahms, Beethoven, and Bach. Likewise, homiletics has its three *B*'s.)

The test of a "great" sermon is not whether the preacher follows the form of another preacher or teacher. The test is whether the sermon does God's work for the hour of its life. If it does, it is a great sermon.

Honesty demands that these statements be made. No other conclusion can be drawn if one studies preaching widely enough to see the varieties of sermons that are produced when mortal men preach. The variations of successful sermons are utterly fantastic. Even more: they are utterly unbelievable.

One more word needs to be added here. There is a second test of the great sermon. This test simply asks, "Can the sermon be improved?" There never has been a sermon written or preached which could not be improved. At this point the lessons taught us by the great preachers—Origen, Augustine, Chrysostom, Luther, Calvin, Spurgeon, Maclaren, Morgan, Truett, Fosdick, Sockman, Sheen, and Graham—serve us well. No great preacher has ever claimed that he reached total perfection in preaching. Indeed, the earnest desire of every great preacher is to be a better preacher. At this point Broadus, Brooks, Blackwood, and many others teach us that it is possible to improve.

Homiletical form is flexible. Search for the best form for yourself. The principles of preaching presented here represent one teacher's approach to preaching. These views are submitted with the conviction that, if tried, they will be found creatively useful.

Question 91: Has your sermon been prepared as a "free," unstructured form from the text and title?

(If it has, you probably have a homily. Unstructured, you will readily recognize, does not mean unprepared. It means the use of a "free" form.)

Question 92: Has your sermon been prepared with an organized introduction, body (normally with two or more points), conclusion, and invitation(s)? (If it has, you probably have a rhetorical sermon.)

See *A Christian Layman's Guide to Public Speaking, Steps to the Sermon,* and *A Quest for Reformation in Preaching* for additional details on these sermon forms.

CHAPTER XI

Your Sermon Style

At this point, take a look at your sermon as a whole. The sermon should be read from beginning to end without stopping to check individual items. In this reading check the style of your sermon.

"Style is the man": so countless teachers and preachers have said. What you say and how you say it are you, and you are your style. More specifically, however, style in preaching relates to three basic elements: (1) clarity, (2) appeal, and (3) force.

Question 93: Has your sermon been prepared so that it is clear from the beginning to end? (If you are not sure, ask someone else to read your sermon. Ask him whether every part of the sermon is clear and understandable. Or you may preach it in private to a friend and ask him to judge how clear it is.)

Question 94: Has your sermon been prepared so that it is appealing from beginning to end? (If so, you are to be congratulated. If you are not sure, check it out as suggested above.)

Question 95: Has your sermon been prepared so as to have force and impact at the key places so that it will "move" people? (If so, congratulations! If you are not sure, check out your sermon.)

POSTSCRIPT

All of us can improve. All of us, as preachers, can surpass our performance in the preparation and delivery of sermons. Every preacher with whom I have talked seriously about preaching earnestly desires to increase the effectiveness of his preaching.

There is some debate about the basic laws of learning. I have heard folks say that the three laws are "repetition, repetition, and repetition"! I have heard others say that the three laws of learning are "work, work, and work"!

If you will accept either of these two sets of learning laws, you not only can wish to improve, you will improve. By making a disciplined effort to improve your homiletical habits for at least one year, you will be astonished at the progress you will make.

You will not be the only beneficiary of such a program of study; your people will benefit. They will rejoice with you over your improvement. They will thank God for the "fresh manna" from their pastor.

You can improve as a preacher. Why don't you?